MARVEL

THE INVINCIBLE IRON MAN

 pi kids® publications international, ltd.

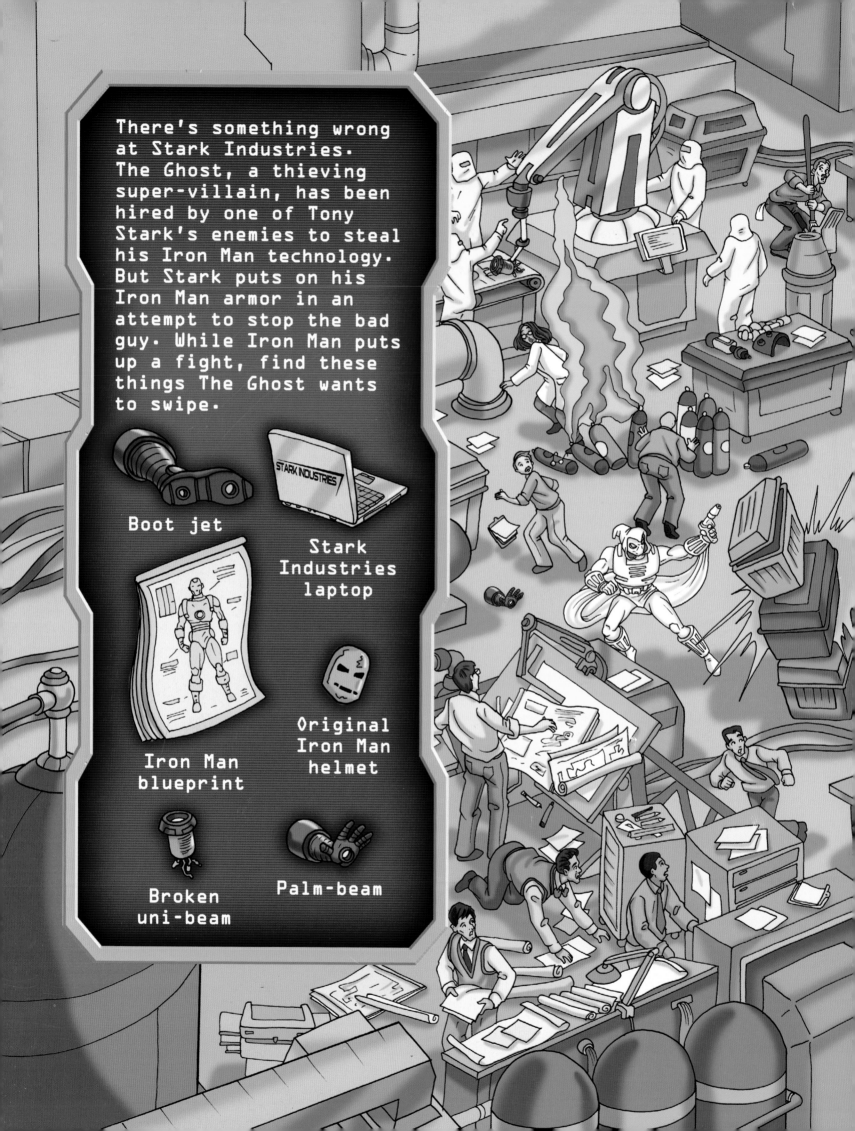

There's something wrong at Stark Industries. The Ghost, a thieving super-villain, has been hired by one of Tony Stark's enemies to steal his Iron Man technology. But Stark puts on his Iron Man armor in an attempt to stop the bad guy. While Iron Man puts up a fight, find these things The Ghost wants to swipe.

Boot jet

Stark Industries laptop

Iron Man blueprint

Original Iron Man helmet

Broken uni-beam

Palm-beam

Did The Mandarin hire The Ghost to burglarize Stark Industries? Iron Man intends to find out. Follow him as he battles his enemy in the high Himalayan Mountains. Then look for these mountaineering items.

Yak horn

Spiked boots

These goggles

Bottled oxygen

Yeti sculpture

Mittens

This rope

This axe

Whiplash wasn't the villain who hired The Ghost to rob Stark Industries. But the Russian bad guy is sure wreaking havoc on Moscow! While Iron Man fights Whiplash, look around for these evil henchmen who are dressed up as famous Russians.

Yuri Gagarin

Mendeleev

Pavlov

Tolstoy

Lenin

Tchaikovsky

Rasputin

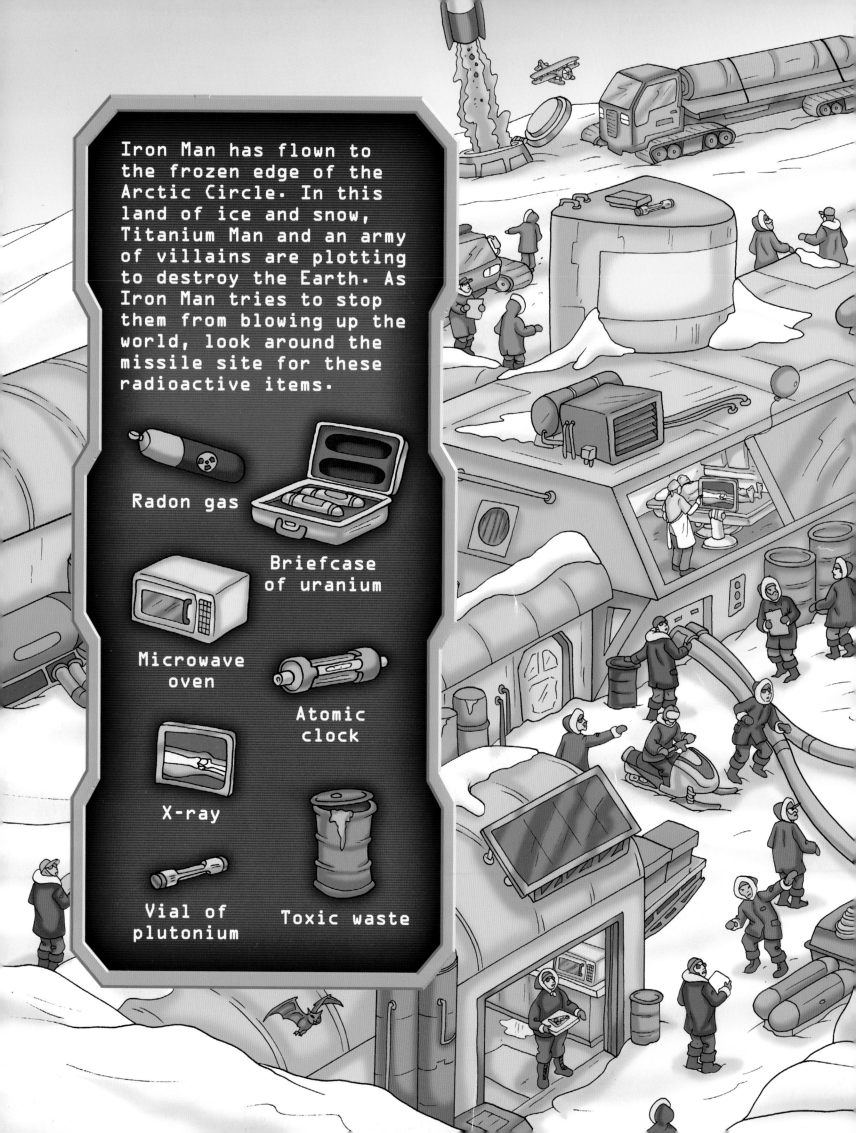

Iron Man has flown to the frozen edge of the Arctic Circle. In this land of ice and snow, Titanium Man and an army of villains are plotting to destroy the Earth. As Iron Man tries to stop them from blowing up the world, look around the missile site for these radioactive items.

Radon gas

Briefcase of uranium

Microwave oven

Atomic clock

X-ray

Vial of plutonium

Toxic waste

At last, Iron Man has found the things that were stolen from Stark Industries, and he knows who hired The Ghost to steal them. It's Doctor Doom, who rules the country of Latveria. Help Iron Man find the stolen items and then put a stop to Doom's evil ways.

Iron Man blueprint

Broken uni-beam

Original Iron Man helmet

Boot jet

Palm-beam

Stark Industries laptop

Iron Man has returned to America only to find that his rival and enemy, Obadiah Stane, has donned his Iron Monger suit. Stane is trying to knock out the city's power in order to leave its citizens helpless and terrified. While Iron Man battles the villain, look for these tools to help fix the damage.

Ratchet

Wrench

Pliers

Hammer

Screwdriver

Welding torch

Break back into Stark Industries and find these frightened employees.

The Mandarin's power comes from his 10 magical rings. Climb back to the Himalayas and find the 10 rings before the villain can.

Motor back to Moscow and look for these things that Whiplash has torn in half with his energy whips.

 Fire hydrant

 Street sign

 Streetlamp

 Bicycle

 Taxi

  Park bench

Cello

Rocket back to Titanium Man's missile site and find these things that fly, just like Iron Man.

 Airplane

 Eagle

 Balloon

Vampire bat

 Kite

 Toy rocket

 Helicopter

Return to Rome and find these faked Italian pieces of art that Count Nefaria's criminals have forged.

The Pieta

Caravaggio's "Boy with a Basket of Fruit"

Mona Lisa

David

Piece of the Sistine Chapel ceiling

The Last Supper

Go back to Latveria and find these old-fashioned items that the country's peasants use while under the reign of Doctor Doom.

Anvil

Lantern

Well

Pitchfork

Wheelbarrow

Wood-fire oven

Butter churn

Make your way back into the electric company and help the manager get to the main switch to restore power to the city.

Head back to Stark Industries and search the crowd for these friends of Iron Man.

Pepper Potts

Rumiko Fujikawa

Jarvis

Happy Hogan

James Rhodes

Bethany Cabe